Secrets of the L

Katrina Dybzynska

First published March 2023 by Fly on the Wall Press
Published in the UK by
Fly on the Wall Press
56 High Lea Rd
New Mills
Derbyshire
SK22 3DP

www.flyonthewallpress.co.uk
ISBN: 9781915789013
Copyright Katrina Dybzynska © 2023

A CIP Catalogue record for this book is available from the British Library.

**With thanks to Aryamati Prize 2022 sponsors:
Elliot J Harper, Kathryn Slattery, Jo Bratten
and Graeme Hall.**

Contents

"Another world is not only possible, she is on her way. On a quiet day, I can hear her breathing."
Arundhati Roy, War Talk

For revolutionaries

The Dictator's Wife on Leaving no Traces

I learnt not to leave traces.
To communicate by smoke signals,
evaporating in the air. To walk as if sweeping
a pine branch behind my footprints.

I remember my grandmother gently repairing
rips in textile she couldn't afford to replace.
She kept her work invisible, carefully selecting
shades and patterns that would blend in.
She always started inside out, hiding the knot.

Her granddaughter, too, is skilled at concealing
the bleeding the needle caused.
Yet, I worry there are too many holes
to keep the threads sealed.

Secrets of the Dictator's Wife

Having secrets is brave when you are a Dictator's
wife. Even the innocent ones — that I let the children stay up
past bedtime, wrote an unsanctioned letter, prayed
to a god not named on the official list of deities.

My secrets need to stay nestled
in my dreams, even if sometimes I wake
to his suspicious stare. It is frightening to think
about them but more terrifying to forget.

There was a time when I was not the Dictator's
Wife, though I am not supposed to talk about it.
Yet I remember. I look back at uncensored
books and thoughts shared sleepily.

A time when the future was more than escape
routes and relentless reminders of loyalties.
The freedom of representing nothing
but my own, not yet final decisions.

The Dictator's Wife Explains the
Order of Things

We are not violent people. We say
please and thank you to our servants.
We tip the discreet waiter and do not reprimand him
for forgetting one of our desserts.

Of course, taking measures is a safety
matter. We practice the social distancing
of nonbelonging worlds. That is the natural
order of things. We are not violent

as violence does not look good
on pictures: it stains. Bloodstains
are not easy to wash off from our expensive cloths
and we respect the people who get to clean them.

We are not violent; we only do what is necessary.
We take no pleasure in setting the barbed wire on top of our wall –
and in hiring its guard (and then another,
to control the first one).

The Dictator's Wife on Cracks

That we drank champagne and ate caviar as luxury
wasn't creative. It was easy to forget we were part
of the constellations when we felt like stars.

The conflicts were never open. A quiet frown
of disapproval, the colors turning pastel.
Straightening of wrinkles and of borders.

Previously drafted sketches became lines
I was not allowed to change. The champagne glasses
held too tight, cracking in my hand.

The Dictator's Wife Watching an Aquarium

He bought it for me but it was he
who spent his life admiring walls.
The key is to make them see-through, he says.
I watch the beautiful creatures, submerged and silent,

and I understand what captivates him.
He admires Siamese fighting fish,
spectacular, combative and so quick
to regenerate.

Maybe they do not remember the ocean.
Perhaps they were bred in laboratories
to his specifications but does that mean
they do not miss the depth?

I want to free them, at least.
I crave to see them
swimming towards the open sea.
I thought you liked fish, he says.

The Dictator's Wife Watching Ships

My Husband thinks the sea should be reserved
for navy fleet, cargo vessels and luxurious yachts.
He can't stand the patience of sailboats.
He enjoys the flags and is comfortable
with the liners that navigate predictable routes,

yet a free-flowing horizon has no place in his calculations.
At least till the next war, when the prospect of conquering
will wake up the explorer in him. He analyses the curve
of losses and gains, though he does not call them losses.
Rather underperforming currents.

He does not hear the storm coming, even if he fears
a change of luck. He would never claim luck,
he plans for the weather. He prefers the reliable structure
of a harbour to the dirt of a beach. He never observes the waves.
That is how I know he will be overthrown.

I like watching the ships disappear. It's so easy
for them to glide out of the picture.

The Dictator's Wife is Taking a Shower

Water always finds a way
to escape. If not as a rebellious
stream then as phantasmal steam.
I used to think evaporating
to be much more graceful
than angry boiling. Now I crave
the hissing of the flames.

The Dictator's Wife Cannot Sleep

Some nights I try to understand
how it feels to be him.

I imagine that I wake up taller, on the other side
of the bed and that is instantly a new perspective.

I picture trimming my moustache with the same absolute
precision I use to sign the military orders.

What do my eyes tell me in the mirror?
Do I notice how tired they seem?

I try to determine where the anger comes from.
I cannot fake his smile.

The only joke he has ever made
was calling me *the only person who sees the Dictator naked.*

Once, I asked if he ever has trouble
falling asleep.

He spoke about his ingenious security measures
and how he keeps his guards in check.

He elaborated on the patrols, arsenals, bunkers,
military strategies and, finally, the gun he keeps under the pillow.

I still try to understand why it is me,
not him, suffering from insomnia.

The Dictator's Wife Turns Away From the Mirror

My mother used to hang long mirrors
in every room so that I would correct
my posture. I stand straight now

yet I do not recognize the face that looks back.
The eyes try to pass a message
but the language they speak is too dangerous to remember.

I have stopped looking since I became a mirror —
shiny, waiting to shatter,
a reflection of someone else.

The Dictator's Wife Gets a Haircut

It's hard to avoid the mirror
when I have to sit here, motionless.
I search beneath

the surface for the self that preceded the Titles.
Mother, the Wife, Your Excellency.
Names can be a weapon.
Mine has been cut off like a teenager's fringe.

I feel sorry for my hair, sculpted in a military
style. No curl can escape. Ironed waves
make an antithesis of the sea. Tightly pulled back knot,
though I am not allowed to look back.

I recall stories in which cutting hair
was a turning point. Samson lost his strength.
Mulan gained invisibility. Some tribes shaved
their heads in mourning.

The spirals on the ground look like serpents.
I remember there are hair styles for times
of peace and haircuts for war.
I tell the hairdresser to keep on cutting.

The Dictator's Wife Receives a Letter From Women From Peaceful Countries

Women from peaceful countries
want to know how one ends up
married to a Dictator.

Like most woman in love I interpreted
the red of the roses as a symbol
of lust, not blood.

Was he easy to become mesmerized by? They want to know.
Women who hate the fathers of their children
ask if he's as uncompromising a Husband

as he is a Leader. Did I want to withdraw?
They demand. In their eyes, that would make me a better
person. Those who don't want to hear my story

say there is a thin line between understanding
and justifying. But they don't see all
the thin lines I balance on.

Women in peaceful countries are quick to judge
silence but in dictatorship even empty banners
shout. Tell the truth, urge those who don't want to hear

how many truths one woman can hold.

Things I Didn't Think I Would do for Love

I knew that love might try me
but I didn't expect for it to take place in court.

I was prepared for love to fade
but not for myself to fade with it.

I was aware that love sometimes makes you
take sides but didn't believe I would be one of them.

It was clear that love makes you say things
you are not sure you still believe

but my love also made me mute
when I didn't believe in silence.

I couldn't be sure that love would last forever
but thought that countries were made of stronger fabric.

The Dictator's Wife on Holiday
(From Metaphors)

For a modern Pharaoh, he does not deal with the Sun
well. We holiday in winter resorts.

No one would take seriously
a sunburnt Dictator, he says.

I laugh.
He does not.

He is good at skiing,
though it is me who lives in parallel lines.

I look at him sliding down a slope
and try to be on vacation from metaphors.

I am not scared of blizzards
but of the muffled steps in snowy silence.

If it is still too sunny, he orders a jet
to misty Scotland.

I like the foggy disappearances
into the distance.

Most of all, I enjoy the cliffs, their final word.
I like arriving at the point where there is no going further.

The Dictator's Wife's Paintings

"Stalin, Mao and Duvalier wrote poetry, Hitler painted and Mussolini played the violin."
Sheila Fitzpatrick

I know about revolutions:
I studied art.

There is nothing more certain than changes
of perception. My favorite masterpiece is *The Treachery*

of Images by Magritte. My husband does not let me
hang it in the bedroom even though he rarely visits there.

He mocks my *little hobby* without realizing
how many secrets you can hide in a painting.

The Dictator and His Wife Watching Guernica

We have seen this painting together.
I saw symbols falling apart.
Deformed pigeon, the parody of peace.
Cracks, chaos, avalanche effect beyond a turning point.

He perceived fame beyond death.
A story of power, strength, justification.
A narrative in which victims are believed to be animals.

I looked at their shock: death always seems to come as a surprise.
Amazed that it is happening now, that we did not bribe
our way out, that there are no second chances.

He noticed the military struggle, heroes protecting their territories.
He nodded to the reason, the eternal order of things.
He only wanted to know — who won?

The Garden of the Dictator's Wife

I did not let the gardeners pluck all the weeds.
I craved their unexpected presence in the palace.
I wanted to watch them resist, bloom, reappear.
Could the Destiny tulips endure the invasion?
I desperately needed to know who would win.

I learnt that the inconspicuous birds-foot trefoils
hide a strong network underground
while the enchanter's nightshades knowingly blossom
in the dimness. Revolutionary poppies
died before they could see their own seeds flowering.

I wondered who gets to decide that they are useless?
Which Flower Dictator chooses the species
with one type of beauty justified more than others?
I witnessed how weeds grew stronger
in spite of that Dictator joining roots.

The Dictator's Wife Asks Questions

Suddenly, I want to know
what is the name of that tree
with starry fruits at the top?
What is this weed that silently
conquers the flower bed?

In whose language
does the mountain stream
take an identity?
Is this hill acknowledged
on any map?

More importantly,
how does a bird returning
from the other side
of the ocean recognize
home?

The Dictator's Wife on the First 15 Minutes of War

I missed the first 15 minutes.
I took a nap and, when I woke up, my bed
was in a battlefield. I got up not in a bedroom
but in a moment of history.

My Husband did not tell me he was going to declare
war but he never tells me anything in advance.
We are at war because we are right, that is all
you need to know, he shrugged.

From the window of our house that has now become a fortress
I watch soldiers trampling my Destiny tulips into the mud.
No one has died yet, so war has not yet turned into a verb.
It is an introduction to a biography that no one ever reads.

Packing children's toys to take to the bunker
I stare at the dolls' glassy eyes fixed to one point
and I cannot track what they see.
I choose my son's bow but not the toy gun.

No one teaches you what should be the first thing
to do when your country has just gone to war,
so I ordered a Bloody Mary and went to change
into trousers.

I wanted to know if that place the dolls watch
might really exist and if it offers asylum.
I missed the first 15 minutes of the war.
I wish I could have missed it all.

The Dictator's Wife Searches for Arrhythmia

I learned to wait
to let muffled screams out.
It's been years now but I studied poppies
and caterpillars. I saw how full of creation
perseverance can be. I learnt to weaponize
endurance. I'm weaving a cocoon
hoping for the layers to amount to a shield.

I'm tired of hope
but not of waiting.
Patience doesn't offer relief
or a conclusion. Yet, I am fluent in the dictator's
song. I know when to foresee arrhythmia.
Why do I expect that I can wait
him out? When the wind changes
direction, there is no stopping waves.

The Dictator's Wife on Silences

In the beginning, it was mysterious.
One paper wrote of it as 'royal'.

Was I tongue-tied or did no one ask honest
questions?

Then it became culpable,
my composed smile taken as support.

Silence is convenient for those who seek
empty containers to drop their words into.

They wouldn't hear when I burned to speak.
Now they wonder how much I knew.

There are different ways of being silenced.
Most of them more subtle than being choked.

Similarly, there are many reasons for keeping quiet.
Most more complex than indifference.

You know that moment when something is slipping out of
your hands and you can still catch it but you suddenly wish

to see it crushed? I am here with some fragile truth
sliding off my tongue.

The Dictator's Wife's Turning Point

The breakthrough happened while I was reading
to the children.

The heroes died as pointlessly
and as frequently as the villains.

I realized I was no Princess any longer
Nor was I ready to live outside the tower.

I became a Witch at the edge of a dark
forest — between it and the palace's manicured garden.

I cultivated tulips and weeds simultaneously.
I created curses but I did not know the saving spells.

I planted labyrinths but grew impatient
and walked through the walls.

Then I thought of dragons
as they, too, are inbetweeners.

The wings do not suffice to claim any bird tribe.
The fish scales are not enough to belong underwater.

I understood why they breathed fire
and where so many tangled heads came from.

When the kids fell asleep, I kept turning pages.
I wanted to know if I'd already passed the turning point.

The Dictator's Wife's Hints at the Disappearance

Houses of Dictators are full of ghosts.
Firstly, you disbelieve.
Later, you see despair taking shape.
Finally, you become one.

The Dictator's Wife's Unsent Report to the Resistance

He is obsessed with road maps that make it easy
to get from A to B. Sometimes he even realizes
there are more letters in the alphabet
but doesn't take into account other dialects.

In moments of passion, he talks about The Pattern
that connects all. Ah, the dream of one code that breaks
all the passwords! He searches for the universal answer
while finding a common question.

He is powerful like those who know no nuance
yet he cannot see the difference between the loyalty
of fear and loyalty to the cause. He takes no risk
so he does not comprehend courage.

He plans many moves ahead but he does not account
for what happens outside the board. He does not expect
the tower to stand on the edge between the squares
or for a black piece to refuse beating the white queen.

He masters pressure and force while skipping
on the resistance and momentum. Mastermind of scare tactics,
territorial antagonisms, unbeatable in his game.
What he does not endure are sudden changes of the rules.

The Dictator's and His Wife's Picture

All morning we try to take this shot.
The Dictator's Wife, usually so well composed,
flinches every time the Dictator
embraces her.

Her trembling smile looks nothing
like the official requirements.
I cannot focus, she apologizes. *Please
not another B&W portrait.*

She asks if the balance and light
are correct but it is the depth
of shadows
she seems to address.

She knows a lot about exposure
and asks for noise reduction.
She cannot wait
to get out of the frame.

There is something blurry
about her, no matter how much I adjust the lens.
Then, I crop out the Dictator
and her face regains contours.

I keep that close-up well hidden. Sometimes
I take it out and zoom in on her eyes.

The Dictator's Dream About Painting

Paint it black and white.
Ban other colors. Apply
only an essence, as diluted
paint will allow for shades
and grey areas. Classify
the brushes. Forbid thin
strokes. Stick strictly
to the official symbols.
Do not leave blank spots.

Paint danger.
Then, in a centre place, a contrasting
solution, just one. Mark clear
lines. Do not let your hand
hesitate — aim for right
angles, no leaks or blurs.
Choose an expensive frame
for your painting to last
in enforced respect.

The Dictator's Journal

Tell them it is temporary. Use the small
print to justify future extensions.
Make it difficult to unsubscribe.
Explain the distinction between danger
outside and the bunker's regulations.
Find a reason hard to argue with — protection,
sacrifice, health. Say we need to unify
our weapons. Give them a sense of purpose
that will turn them into accomplices.
Do not move the line, just stretch it.
When it snaps, it will fall in a place
you aimed for all along. Claim it an accident.

The Dictator's Wife Doesn't Support the Revolution

I wake up
in a place I can't recognize.
Jail or asylum? I am calm
like those who survived.

I don't support the revolution
as it requires having nothing else to lose.
Will I testify against the man
who, at times, seemed to be a part of me?

Author Biography

Katrina Dybzynska is a nomadic writer published internationally (among others, Mslexia, the London Reader, Poethead, Fly on the Wall Press, Lucent Dreaming) and awarded in 20 competitions. She is a BA-MA Researcher at Global Centre for Advanced Studies. She is passionate about the narratives of ecopoetry, uncivilisation and decolonization. She likes to write from the edges, usually of the Irish cliffs she parks her campervan too close to.

She also runs wild creativity retreats in Andalusia: https://katdybzynska.wixsite.com/page

Acknowledgements

No book is an island. Secrets of the Dictator's Wife belongs to an archipelago of the research on psychology of power and to the sea of activism poetry.

This book owes a lot to some of the revolutionaries in my life:

Thank you, Creston Davis, for letting me work on this project as a part of my BA, saving me from writing some academic thesis that we both know I would fail in.

Thank you, Eileen Brannigan, for being one of the first ones to believe in the Dictator's Wife and for telling me when she was becoming infuriating.

Thank you, Isabelle Kenyon, for your unfailing enthusiasm and your patience when I was re-editing the edits.

Thank you to my wonderful, smart, and handsome partner who is sitting across the table from me but I am still supposed to put it here, right?

Thank you to the editors of the publications where some of those poems found home for the first time:

Dictator's and His Wife's picture was first accepted by Mslexia.

The Dictator's Wife watching ships was printed in Fly on the Wall Press magazine.

The Dictator's Wife Cannot Sleep appeared in POETRY in the TIME of CORONAVIRUS.

The Dictator's dream about painting could be first read in Dear Leader Tales anthology, Feral Cat Publishers.

About Fly on the Wall Press

A publisher with a conscience.

Political, Sustainable, Ethical.

Publishing politically-engaged, international fiction, poetry and cross-genre anthologies on pressing issues. Founded in 2018 by founding editor, Isabelle Kenyon.

Some other publications:

The Sound of the Earth Singing to Herself by Ricky Ray

We Saw It All Happen by Julian Bishop

*Odd as F*ck by Anne Walsh Donnelly*

Imperfect Beginnings by Viv Fogel

These Mothers of Gods by Rachel Bower

Sin Is Due To Open In A Room Above Kitty's by Morag Anderson

Snapshots of the Apocalypse by Katy Wimhurst

Demos Rising

Exposition Ladies by Helen Bowie

A Dedication to Drowning by Maeve McKenna

The House with Two Letterboxes by Janet H Swinney

Climacteric by Jo Bratten

Cracked Asphalt by Sree Sen

Social Media:

@fly_press (Twitter) @flyonthewall_poetry (Instagram)

@flyonthewallpress (Facebook)

www.flyonthewallpress.co.uk